D1525465

A PARENT'S GUIDE TO STRING INSTRUMENT STUDY

Helpful Information For Families With
Children Studying
Orchestral String Instruments

WS3

$2.50

kjos
west

Neil A. Kjos, Jr., Publisher   San Diego, CA and Park Ridge, IL

©1977 KJOS WEST, San Diego, California
Published by Kjos West
Distributed by Neil A. Kjos Music Company
National Order Desk
4382 Jutland Drive, San Diego, California 92117

International Standard Book Number 0-8497-5700-2
Library of Congress Card Number 77-79565
Printed and Bound in the United States of America
Edition Number WS3

TABLE OF CONTENTS

ONE

THE INTRODUCTION

"Neither my husband nor I know anything about music. What are our son's chances for learning an instrument?

"We are a little afraid of starting a string instrument; they look so fragile and complicated!"

"I understand the first few years are an excruciating experience for the whole family. Is that true?"

"Is the violin really the hardest instrument to learn how to play?"

When one boy bows another's violin, seriousness and fun combine to stimulate learning.

If thoughts like these have been in your mind as you contemplated starting your child on a string instrument, at least be assured that you are normal! Few parents enter into such an undertaking with complete confidence of success, even if they happen to own a violin or cello and have played themselves.

Your apprehensions may be real or imagined. In any case, becoming familiar with the instrument, the course of study, and what is expected of you and your child will give you more confidence and perhaps a touch of optimism!

During the past decade I have been teaching the Suzuki method which brings me into contact with the parents on a regular basis. Many of the beginning children in this system are not yet in first grade, which means the parent must assume complete responsibility for the instrument as well as the daily training which takes place at home. Naturally many of them feel inadequate at first.

So that they will not transmit their tensions and insecurities to the children, group parent's sessions precede or run concurrently with the child's first lessons. At this time, the parent experiences the first steps in learning to play the violin, becomes acquainted with those aspects of the string instrument with which he will have to deal, and discusses the common concerns of practice, attitude, motivation and personal relationships.

These sessions have taught me a lot about what parents would like to know. Periodic get-togethers, which include the parents of older students, the exchange of comments, ideas, and questions, has made it clear that families share similar problems no matter what their background.

Unfortunately, comprehensive parent orientation meetings are the exception rather than the rule. The best and busiest of teachers may find that such events are the least pressing item in a hectic schedule.

Even if you felt well informed at the beginning of the semester, what would you do on the first day of Christmas vacation when the A string breaks and your child's teacher is out of town until after your child is due to play his solo in church? Could you use a "How To Change A String" chapter? (See "Care and Maintenance of String Instruments", Chapter 11).

For my own students' parents, and for all who need encouragement, information and inspiration, the following material has been compiled. It is designed to be elementary and helpful. However, it will also refer you to other writings which may be more eloquent and comprehensive than this volume can or intends to be.

If you personally feel more confident with *A Parents' Guide To String Instrument Study* in your hands, its purpose will be accomplished.

TWO

THE OVERTURE

An Introduction to the Parent's Role

Many factors will influence the degree of success that your child experiences in his study of a string instrument. As a concerned parent you would like to believe that it is within your power to regulate these factors, but it is only realistic to acknowledge that the older the child, the less *direct* control you can effectively exert.

Obviously, the parent's role is one of extreme importance no matter how old the child. Your part, however, will vary with the child's age, and it will change as the child grows in years as well as in musicianship.

If your child is still very young, perhaps pre-school through second grade, there is little question that his interest and accomplishment depend almost totally on you. This is quite a responsibility, but a good teacher can guide you in setting the home environment, developing a practice routine, and using the best psychology. You will experience rewards in the joy of learning and sharing together through this early start that can never be duplicated.

As the student's age increases, your influence should become more subtle, although not obscure. The importance you give to music in your life will be observed by your children as are the other values you hold. Your child will notice, for instance, without having it pointed out to him that you have chosen to attend a music program requiring considerable effort in terms of time, transportation and dress, rather than to sit in front of the television set.

The role of the parent can be viewed as encompassing three general areas:

1) Financial
2) Practical
3) Psychological

It has been pointed out already that these roles will be in an almost continuous state of change depending on the child's most urgent needs at a given moment. These needs are tempered by age and musical maturity.

In the Financial category, the need for the following items occurs and re-occurs. To the best of your ability they should be provided willingly and when needed. These items are discussed in more detail in other sections of this book.

1) INSTRUMENT: The quality and price will probably continue to increase along with the student's ability!
2) ACCESSORIES: Strings need periodical replacement; music stands, shoulder pads, mutes and other items make playing easier or more pleasant.
3) MUSIC: This will be selected by the teacher in the early years of study.
4) MAINTENANCE - REPAIR: Bows need rehairing when recommended by the teacher. String instruments are surprisingly sturdy and need minimal attention. When something goes awry, however, it must have immediate attention.
5) LESSONS: Public school instruction is usually free; private or small group lessons from professional teachers are available at a wide range of fees
6) RECORDINGS: These are required in only a few methods, but are becoming accepted as an effective means of developing a musical sense and appreciation.

The Practical category would include a wide variety of items such as:

1) TRANSPORTATION: This means being available on a regular basis to provide rides to lessons and rehearsals. It could involve festivals, contests and special occasions.
2) MUSICAL PROBLEMS: Even with a limited background in music, you can probably help your child work through a notation or rhythm problem.
3) INSTRUMENT PROBLEMS: Tuning a string instrument daily is important and parents can help. Making a minor repair such as changing a string or setting a bridge is easier for an adult.

4) SCHEDULES: Depending on age, your child may need help in anticipating lesson conflicts, keeping a practice schedule, following through with an assignment, or just remembering when the instrument must be taken with him!

Even if all of the above provisions are furnished, unless the essential human ingredients of personal involvement and concern are included, the investment of time and money may be wasted. Children are extremely perceptive. If your interest in his musical training is superficial, so also will be your child's. Your first reluctance to provide the supportive items above will be clearly read, and with a little persistence he can rid himself of that bothersome responsibility of practice and music lessons.

If you sincerely believe that the training you hope to provide for your child is essential for his full enjoyment of what life and our culture have to offer, he will feel it. If, on the other hand, you are what has been called a "stage mother" with unwarranted expectations of what your Johnny can accomplish, or if the music lessons mean status in your social group, that too will be sensed.

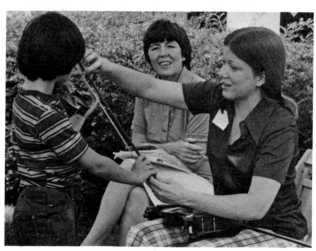

A parent attending the child's lesson, whether indoors or out, should sit quietly nearby taking notes and observing how to help the child at home if necessary.

Personal or psychological support may have as its beginning your motives for providing the musical training, but its limits are set only by your willingness to understand the needs of your child as he progresses through his study. One day you will have to deal with the vehement declaration that he abhors the instrument, will have no more of it, and hates you for making him play it. On another day you may find yourself dancing around the kitchen floor with an exuberant young performer who reports that he held his class spellbound for twenty minutes with his demonstration of musical knowledge and ability.

Most situations fall somewhere inbetween. Because of their scope, the only sure preparation for events which lie ahead is to have a clear view of your motives, a working knowledge of psychology, and an attitude which is at all times positive!

Your Goals

Therefore, be ready to accept as top priority in your role as a parent the major responsibility for providing:
1) MOTIVATION: Furnish environment and stimulation which leads the child forward on his own volition.
2) ENCOURAGEMENT AND SUPPORT: Be generous with your praise and find ways to show your sincere interest.
3) SYMPATHY AND ASSISTANCE: Listen to your child's comments and make recommendations. Evaluate problems considering all possible influences. Seek outside help if needed.
4) A POSITIVE APPROACH which will influence the way you handle all situations, and will be passed on to your child helping him to attain a healthy attitude toward music in general and problems in particular.

THREE

INTRODUCING THE INSTRUMENTS

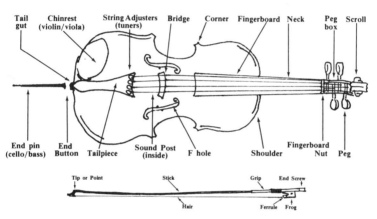

Tail gut   Chinrest (violin/viola)   String Adjusters (tuners)   Bridge   Corner   Fingerboard   Neck   Peg box   Scroll

End pin (cello/bass)   End Button   Tailpiece   Sound Post (inside)   F hole   Shoulder   Fingerboard Nut   Peg

Tip or Point   Stick   Grip   End Screw

Hair   Ferrule   Frog

THE STRING FAMILY

Stringed instruments are among the oldest known to man. They may have one string or dozens, and be plucked, bowed or hammered.

The string instruments known as the orchestral family are those which composers have included in ensemble music of our Western culture since before the 17th century. There are four basic members— the violin, viola, violoncello (usually referred to as cello, rhyming with Jello), and double bass (prounounced base, and originally called bass viol). It is also frequently called string bass or simply bass.

When people speak of studying a stringed instrument they are usually referring to one of the orchestral family even though there are several other popular instruments having strings such as guitar, harp and piano. Because the bowed string instruments are so tremendously versatile, they have remained popular through the years. They can sustain tones, play chords, be plucked, produce any pitch, sound percussive or sweet, and endless combinations of all of these. No wonder they are also a favorite of composers and arrangers.

Shape

Members of the orchestral family have come to us in essentially the same shape for about four centuries, having evolved from the family of ancient bowed instruments called viols. They share a distinctive silhouette known as the "violin shape". The dimensions are somewhat different from one to the other, and even vary slightly between almost identical instruments, depending on the maker.

The double bass actually has two standard shapes, one very similar to the violin, the other more resembling the ancient viol family with very sloping shoulders which extend from the side of the neck, and corners in the mid-section which do not flair like those of the violin.

Tone Qualities

The four different instruments have voices which can be compared to a vocal quartet of soprano, alto, tenor and bass. Although each instrument is now manufactured in several sizes to accommodate young students, each size has its strings tuned to the pitch - or sound - of the "full-sized" instrument.

The violin is capable of producing the highest sounds in the orchestra and it is frequently given a melodic line. Its singing, high register carries beautifully. This makes it a fine instrument for solos. Many more violins are used in the traditional orchestra than each of the other strings, and they are usually divided into two sections. Because of its popularity, more students tend to begin on violin than on the other strings.

Sounding five tones lower than the violin is the viola. To enhance its deeper pitch, the viola is larger than the violin by one to three inches, depending on the length of the viola. More small violas are available now than years ago since more young students are interested in beginning on them. With its alto-tenor quality voice, the viola adds depth to the sound of the orchestra and string quartet, and its solo passages tend to be warm and rich.

Held between the knees of a seated player, the cello is also supported by an end pin securely positioned on the floor. Its strings are tuned one ocatve (eight tones) below the viola. Its bow is relatively heavier to be effective on the thicker and deeper sounding strings. The cellist is frequently called upon during featured passages to play material as technically demanding as the violinist. A melody played by the entire cello section of an orchestra is always favorably received.

Furnishing a most essential foundation to the orchestral sound is the double bass, so called because it sounds an octave lower than the notes it is reading. In recent years, players have given it a place on the solo stage, but it remains primarily the solid "bottom" of the orchestral string section. The bass enjoys a versatility, however, which is not quite matched by its relatives. It is a star in the jazz field, welcomed in the concert band, often included in chamber music, and its players can transfer to electric bass guitar with a little practice!

OBTAINING AN INSTRUMENT

Once it has been decided which instrument the student will play, it is important to know with whom he will be studying, at least in the beginning stages. This plays a significant role in how one goes about obtaining an instrument.

If your child is entering a school program:
1) You may have an opportunity to rent or borrow an instrument from the school.
2) You might receive a letter of information from the school which outlines the options available to you in getting an instrument, and listing the local music stores that have them for rent or purchase.
3) Cellos and basses are frequently owned by the school since their cost might discourage a family from starting unless an instrument were readily available.

If your child is enrolling for private lessons:
1) The teacher will want to meet with you and your child to ascertain exactly what size the instrument should be.
2) Your teacher will discuss with you the options available and probably make some personal recommendations as to dealers and quality.
3) The teacher may act as an intermediary between you and a family that has an instrument for sale which fits your requirements.

If you are enrolling in a Suzuki program:
1) Many teachers want the parent to learn to play before the child. Teachers differ as to whether the adult needs an instrument other than the child's while becoming acquainted with the beginning techniques.
2) Very small instruments may not be stocked by the local instrument dealers, and your teacher will tell you how new instruments are ordered.
3) Areas with established Suzuki programs frequently form a network for instrument "swapping" among families, since young beginners may need a larger instrument in a year or two and many dealers are reluctant to take little instruments in on trade for strictly economic reasons.

It is not uncommon for a child to be urged to study an instrument because there happens to be one available, perhaps in the attic, or offered by a relative. If the child is enthusiastic over this situation, you have taken at least one small step towards deciding on an instrument. But do not breathe freely too soon. There are many things yet to consider.

SIZE

The most frequent injustice beset upon young string players is to furnish them with an instrument which is an improper size. Although it is a serious error regardless of the kind of instrument, it is especially critical for violin and viola players.

Students are told to support the instrument, to varying degrees, with the shoulder or collarbone area. With arm extended, they must then round their fingers over the top of the fingerboard of the instrument to depress the string downward with the *fingertip.* This becomes an agonizing posture if the arm is extended its full length causing the elbow to be relatively straight and requiring the wrist to bend at almost a 90 degree angle in order to position the fingers properly.

So the child adjusts to the discomfort by lowering his arm so it is supported a little by his ribs, and he points the violin downward. It also usually comes to the direct front of the player (not good) and alters the position of the bowing so that the bow easily slips downward over the fingerboard (also not good). In addition, he allows his fingers to flop on their soft pads to avoid the muscle strain.

Cello is popular, as shown by this group concert at the Suzuki Institute, Stevens Point, Wisconsin.

Thus from a violin which is too large we get a good share of all the problems which discourage beginners and create dropouts— discomfort in playing, poor position to develop any facility, weak or poor tone, sloppy appearance, and many bad habits virtually impossible to correct, with grace, at a later date.

Assure your teacher that you are anxious to have an insrument which fits the child *now,* small enough for ease of playing yet as large as possible for a full-bodied tone.

- 14 -

RENTAL OR PURCHASE?

Most people who rent string instruments do so because they are not confident that the student will "like it", referring to playing. They feel that the instrument then can be returned with a minimum of complication or money wasted. This may indeed be true, but before you decide to rent or purchase outright there are several things for you to consider.

Time

Learning to play a string instrument to bring pleasure to yourself and others is within the capabilities of virtually everyone, but it does take time. Most shops which have instruments for rent have a Rental-Purchase Plan whereby you rent the instrument for a specified number of months, after which, if you decide to buy it, the rental money is applied to the purchase price. These plans differ greatly, but most begin with a three month minimum rental.

Unfortunately, about the time the first rental contract has been fulfilled, the student might be feeling discouraged, or a parent may be disappointed in the "results" or apparent lack of dedication. The instrument gets returned and it is all over—or is it, really?

A family which recognizes the value of music making in a young person's life should make a commitment to at least one year of study. Avoid giving yourself the option of getting out easily. Once such a commitment has been made, one can evaluate the financial attributes of rental over purchase from a new perspective.

Attitude

Consider the less tangible elements. Having an instrumental outfit which really belongs to you and is not just borrowed from a store can give the student his own feeling of pride in ownership. He is more likely to care for it so it will look new longer. Also, spoken or not, he will know that someone is confident that he will be a success in his new undertaking.

Quality

Another aspect to consider about renting would involve the quality of the instrument. Your dealer probably has a specific student model which is for rent. If it is in good adjustment—that is, falling within specifications set down by reputable instrument makers and music educators—it could be acceptable for a beginner. However, there are shortcomings to an inexpensive student instrument and they might be such that the delight of learning becomes a chore. Difficulties encountered of a technical nature may actually originate with the instrument or bow, whereas they would not exist in an instrument of slightly higher quality.

In addition, if your beginner sticks with it you will probably want to consider stepping up in quality after a year or so. Would you dare to be optimistic and start out with a better quality instrument to begin with?

If renting is the best way to cope with the financial aspects of beginning the study of an instrument, by all means go ahead with it and do not wait until a later date when things might possibly be "easier". The earlier a child begins on a string instrument, the more rewarding it will be for everyone involved. This has a physical basis as well as psychological, and the beginning should not be delayed.

SELECTING AN INSTRUMENT

If you are renting, your choice of an instrument may be limited but you can check on the various rental plans by phone. You could also ascertain the retail value of the rental outfits and whether they are new or pre-owned instruments.

Purchasing an instrument, on the other hand, means you will have a wide variety from which to choose. Price will play some part in your choice. You are no doubt aware that you could pay well into the thousands of dollars, but whatever your limit you will find a good value if you look at several instruments and get the advice of a teacher specializing in strings.

Kinds of Business

Several kinds of businesses may be available to you when it comes time to select an instrument.
1) The large music store which carries virtually everything from sheet music and pianos to small instruments and music stands.
2) The instrument store which specializes in band and orchestra instruments and their accessories.
3) The specialty shop known as the Violinmakers, which sells orchestral string instruments, their accessories, does repairs.
4) The mail order business, some specializing in string instruments and supplies.

Outfits

For the student in the elementary stages outfits are available which include the instrument, bow, case and usually some rosin for the bow. As the student becomes more advanced he will want to select each component to suit his taste.

Before you shop, read about the various parts of the instruments. Then you will be able to look at an instrument and evaluate it, or at least know what to ask about.

If the student is a beginner there are several positive things you can observe or ask about the instrumental outfit:

1) Is the instrument equipped with chrome-wound steel "sensitive" strings?
2) Does it have four string adjusters? Possibly only two for cello, none for bass.
3) Do the pegs turn easily and stay in place?
4) Is the case waterproof and sturdy with secure fasteners and a compartment with cover to hold rosin, strings, etc.?
5) Is the bow straight when sighting from screw to tip along the top?
6) Does the bow stick feel strong and solid when the hair is tightened yet maintaining its inward arch? (This might have to be left to the judgement of the teacher.)
7) Is the outfit equipped with rosin and a pitchpipe?

When You Buy

The value of an instrument is determined by many factors, and if you are making a purchase, particularly of a full size that you expect to have around for awhile, a number of those factors should be considered.

An instrument's tone quality is obviously very important. Although certain aspects of the tone can be altered by different strings, or a readjustment of bridge or sound post, the intrinsic quality of the instrument will remain. An ideal way to judge the sound is to have a good player perform on it. Listen for a clear resonant tone. It is always valuable to have two or more instruments played so that they can be compared.

Physical appearance can affect the price. If the varnish is particularly unattractive, or badly marred, an instrument will sell for less even though it may possess a lovely tone.

A reputable violinmaker will not offer an instrument for sale unless it has been adjusted to the best of his ability. If, however, you are buying from some other source you will want to look the instrument over carefully and get your teacher's impression. Check for noticeable open cracks in top and back, and see if there are any of the glued seams open. This would cause buzzing when the instrument is played.

The Attic Violin (or Viola or Cello)

Publicity about a rare violin by an old master found in the dark recesses of an attic has frequently sent the family running to the violinmaker in the nearest city with great-granddad's instrument containing the Stradivarius label. It is true that valuable instruments have been located in long-forgotten storage places, but the possibility of them being worth large sums of money is slight.

Nonetheless, if you have an instrument which has been in the family for three generations or more, you will probably be interested in what your violinmaker can tell you about it. If you wish to know its value, you must be prepared to pay the appraiser a percentage of what he says it's worth since his time and opinions constitute his business.

If you are considering its use for your child, there are several things to check to be sure it will contribute to his musical enjoyment and not hinder it.

1) Be certain that your child is ready for that particular size.
2) Have a violinmaker examine it for soundness of construction, seeing that everything is firmly glued and that it meets the measurement specifications of modern instruments, including bridge adjustments.
3) Have a complete set of new strings put on with accompanying string adjusters.
4) Furnish a chinrest, for violins, that suits your child.
5) Frequently the bow must be replaced totally. If it is judged sound by the appraiser, it will at least need new bow hair.
6) Ancient cases may not protect the instrument in modern lifestyle. They may also be uncomfortable to carry and present a negative image to your child's friends (at least in his eyes). Consider a new case.

FOUR

TYPES OF INSTRUCTION

The Lesson

The decision to learn to play a string instrument usually follows an appealing presentation given by a teacher or a performer. It is desirable to have the prospective student express an interest in learning to play the instrument rather than having it decided for him by an adult. Ways to bring this about are discussed in the chapter on motivation.

While the initial interest is fresh it is wise to consider the possibility of beginning lessons. As time passes, interest will wain if activity is not taking place. You almost surely will be able to boast, "It's good we didn't start violin because he's not the slightest bit interested now!"

Rather, begin while there is an urge to do so. If most of the necessary factors are present in the classroom and home, the student's initial enthusiasm will carry him through the demanding early lessons. The skill he acquires there will serve him well as he recognizes the need for increased application and repetition in order to reach his goals.

PUBLIC SCHOOL STRING PROGRAMS

A common form of recruitment is that which occurs in the public schools. If aptly handled by the teacher, it can bring a flood of enrollees. If presented in an unimaginative way, it can make membership in the string class about as appealing as appointment to the clean-up committee for after the ball game!

Types of learning situations offered by individual school districts vary greatly. Budget considerations usually make private lessons impractical. Some schools are able to teach groups of students all learning the same instrument in the same class. Other schools may take all of the string family (violin, viola, cello and bass) in one heterogenous class. There are advantages to each approach.

Factors which determine how your particular public school program operates include such considerations as the age of the beginners, needs of the existing orchestra program, available time of the teacher, physical facilities, and the number of students who want to begin.

Beautiful weather gives this violin class a chance to take a musical stroll between periods of concentrated work.

Several things make starting lessons on a string instrument at school attractive:

1) Friends are usually involved and it is more fun to learn together.
2) Often times the school has instruments which can be used or rented.
3) Scheduling in or adjacent to school hours makes extra travel to lessons unnecessary.
4) If the class consists of representatives of each string instrument, one gains knowledge and appreciation of their attributes, problems, and the place they play within the orchestra.

As we might expect, there are corresponding difficulties which the public school string student will face:

1) Group and Individual Progress: It is inevitable that individual differences will surface quickly regarding the skills being developed in the class. Although a well-trained teacher can do much to keep every child challenged, there is bound to be grumbling from some about the progress of others. Unfortunately, it is often the better students who decide to withdraw.
2) If the school furnishes your child with an instrument, it must be in good repair and adjustment. School budgets are often

inadequate in this department and your teacher finds it necessary to exercise priorities. Have the borrowed instrument check by a qualified violinmaker (servicing all string instruments) for recommendations.

3) Scheduling Problems: The class might be too large, too mixed, too infrequent, or held during a vital academic period that your child cannot miss. The class might fall too early before school or too late after school. It may have to be held in the furnace room or the hallway because there's no other room! If it is in the music room, it is not unusual to have other students practicing in another corner of the room simultaneously, particularly in open classroom or modular schedules.

4) Specialization: When a child pulls well ahead of his group he may face the additional frustration of seeking help that his teacher, who may not be a string specialist, finds difficult to give. Orchestra and band teachers are usually required to perform on and teach all standard instruments at a high level, which is a formidable objective, especially if violins came into your life at a very late date!

THE PRIVATE LESSON

Although the advantages of group learning in music are recognized, the highly motivated student may soon want to augment his school instruction with lessons from a private teacher.

A private lesson implies that the teacher will instruct the student in a studio where the two of them are alone. This is usually to the exclusion of parents, too. If you want to attend some or all of the lessons, be sure that this is understood and arranged in advance.

Even though some teachers are extremely versatile on several instruments, it is desirable to study with one whose major is that instrument about which you want to learn. Lessons from a reputable teacher will give the student an optimum chance of success, at least technically, on his instrument. The development of musicianship and the motivation to practice will be influenced by many other factors in addition to the teacher.

The cost of instruction varies greatly, from a token payment to a promising college student, to the highly professional fee charged by an artist-teacher.

One advantage of the private lesson is the undivided attention of an expert. This, for a price, gives a feeling of assurance that all is being done as correctly as possible. Assignments will be geared to the individual student's needs for maximum progress.

Private lessons are not the "cure-all" for weak or disinterested students. Even with the beginning students, much responsibility must be accepted by the families involved to create an environment which places importance on musical achievement and the rewards of study. Even with private lessons, the student who practices very little will accomplish very little.

Studying privately cannot substitute for the joy of sharing music with others in group performance, even if it is at an elementary level. To fill a need for interaction among students, some teachers hold informal class meetings in addition to a more formal periodic recital. At these, the students play for one another, perhaps including parents, in a more relaxed atmosphere than the annual concert.

SMALL GROUP LESSONS

Filling a need which might be financial as well as psychological are those lessons given in small groups of the same instrument. Your public school may be able to offer these, but more often the role is assumed by conservatories or schools of music.

Students unquestionably learn from observing one another and it is often comforting to share the difficulties of an assignment with others. Depending, of course, on the situation and the teacher, students might find lessons more tension-free and be more motivated to practice with the possibility of recognition from classmates.

As in many group situations, students are frequently held to a common rate of progress. It is not unusual to limit this type of introduction to an instrument to one year, with the understanding that the student will then enroll for private lessons.

SUZUKI METHOD: CHILD AND PARENT

Since the mid-1960's the Suzuki approach has been building in popularity and has been adapted to a variety of teaching situations. The elements which constitute the most obvious departure from the traditional methods are 1) the recommended pre-school beginning age; 2) the extended rote approach, and 3) the involvement of a parent or other adult who will guide the child's practice at home.

What usually receives little emphasis is that it embraces an entire philosophy of education which can be utilized by the children and their families in other subjects.

By definition, the Suzuki system is the development of musical skills in children essentially in the same way in which they learned their native language. Suzuki calls this the Mother Tongue approach.

Suzuki training, which is fashioned along prescribed lines, advocates starting a child on violin or cello as early as possible, preferably by the age of four. This relates directly to the system of teaching and the way in which young children learn. The method is most effective when started at the pre-school age. Selected aspects of the method are valid at any age or level.

A parent attends the lessons and may actually be learning to play along with the child in order to be a more effective daily teacher at home.

A certain level of technical ability is attained before the student's attention is directed to the reading of notes. A recording of the pieces to be studied furnishes the student with a concept of violin tone in addition to familiarizing him with the elements of the music (melody, rhythm, accompaniment, intonation, phrasing, etc.). This, in combination with the help of teacher and parent, constitutes the core of his instruction.

Lessons in the Suzuki method are always individual in nature, but not necessarily private. This means several children and parents may be observing the lesson of another. Additional instruction, motivation, and fun are acquired at the group sessions which are held periodically, perhaps each week or less frequently.

For the parent or teacher interested in the Suzuki approach, detailed reading material is available. Consult "Suggested Reading" found on page 69.

FIVE

HOW TO CHOOSE A TEACHER

If other than public school instruction has been decided upon, finding "the right teacher" may well be worth the time and effort it could take. Comparatively few families are fortunate enough to have chosen to study a string instrument primarily because they first found an outstanding program and teacher.

Use the following suggestions as a starting point for locating and selecting a teacher:

1) If your child has a friend who is studying, ask the parents for their reaction to the teacher. Find out if the student goes to lessons happily, if he practices willingly when reminded, and if he sounds well when he shares his music. Get the parent's evaluation of the approach used by the teacher. Find out what programs have been given during the year and the general impression that the other students have made.

2) Contact a nearby college, conservatory, or music school for what instruction is available. In addition to fees, you should learn if a teacher has a preference for certain age and levels. The school may make a recommendation, in which case it would be to your advantage to talk with the teacher, preferably in person. Evaluate his personality with your child in mind, and his professional approach to the best of your ability. Schools tend to have frequent performance programs where you could see and hear examples of the teacher's product.

3) Consult with the public school instrumental music teacher or music supervisor. Some keep a list of available instructors.

Beware of the overly versatile teacher who will teach anyone anything. A specialist in one of the "families" of instruments (brass, woodwind, strings, or percussion) may serve you well in his chosen area, but further diversity on the teacher's part may not produce the quality you are looking for in a private lesson.

4) Music stores which carry instruments and supplies might suggest a person who teaches at the store. Keep in mind that sales are still the primary function of a music store, and that a teacher on the staff should still be checked out carefully using the ways suggested above.

5) In the specialized area of teaching the Suzuki method, the above suggestions apply but additional information is needed. Particular attention must be paid to the personality of the teacher since dealing with the young child is an art in itself, and the addition of violin study requires quite a special individual to be a fine teacher.

It is not uncommon to call oneself a "Suzuki Teacher" on the grounds that a few of the method's ideas are incorporated into the course of study, when in reality there has been no official training and the fundamental elements of Suzuki's philosophy scarcely exist. If your prospective teacher is a member of the Suzuki Association of the Americas, he should know what training and updating is recommended.

The Suzuki Association will furnish upon request the names of persons in your area or state who are teachers or who can direct you to known teachers in your area. They will also supply pamphlets outlining what to look for in a program to be assured it is following the Suzuki approach. Briefly, some of those aspects include:

1) Individual lessons plus group sessions.
2) Postponement of reading until technic on the instrument is developed and readiness is established.
3) Emphasis on listening to recordings.
4) Creative teaching using the materials within the method.
5) Continuous review, reinforcement and performance of learned works.
6) Cooperation rather than competition among students.

POINTS TO CONSIDER
ABOUT TEACHERS AND LESSONS

Scheduling

Lessons should be at regular intervals, usually once a week. Avoid frequent or extended "vacation" time since it tends to give the student the feeling that daily practice can also be suspended. As a result, the feel for the instrument diminishes, routine is broken, and what seems comfortable before the break is now frustratingly difficult.

Few teachers will schedule lessons on an every-other-week basis, even though some parents may think it advisable. In truth, unless the student is an adult, a weekly check on the direction of study is only sensible. It would be disastrous to continue to practice something incorrectly for an extended period, particularly since it will take twice as long to correct it!

Teacher Linda MacRury of Philadelphia, Pa., helps establish the proper hand position in a young student in order to avoid remedial work later.

In addition, experience has shown that bi-weekly lessons for children at the early levels results in waining interest and less than half the progress.

Qualifications and Cost

Since you are making an investment of time, energy, and dedication in addition to the cost of supplying an instrument, you should seek the best possible instruction within your financial means. The most expensive teacher may not be the best for your child when considering his age and advancement. Nor is a very "reasonable" teacher by any means a bargain. You might find a teacher at half the usual cost, but be prepared to learn half as much and take twice the time to do it!

There is frequently a correlation between the fee charged by a teacher and his performing ability. This is understandable since artistry is a scarce commodity and certainly much hard work and financial outlay has been involved. But caution must be exercised not to assume that great technique and musicianship means superior teaching. Although there may be an advantage to having a virtuoso for a teacher, it is much more important that he possess good basic musicianship and an enthusiasm for teaching.

It is helpful if a teacher can demonstrate well for a student at the lesson. But for the beginning student the primary consideration should be that the teacher's personality is warm and sympathic, and that he be thoroughly familiar and skilled with elementary teaching techniques and the problems encountered by beginners.

Most specialized teachers of string instruments aspired, at one time or another, to be professional performers, not necessarily solo artists but respected members of reputable concert groups. Along the way, many of them discovered that teaching could be rewarding and pleasurable, and made an effort to develop both careers and now successfully combine them.

Others find themselves in playing positions less than that to which they aspired, and teaching has become a sideline that must be endured to support themselves. Frequently these teachers are ineffective.

A modest performer who early set his goals on teaching as a speciality may well surpass an impressive concert artist in helping others learn the techniques of playing an instrument. Results are what count, and a teacher in any field needs to communicate on the personal level and draw from an abundant supply of professional subject matter.

Recommendations on Material Goods

The teacher will be the judge of what method and books are to be used. You should be prepared to purchase updated materials and not expect those from years ago to suffice.

Another area of teacher responsibility is to assist you with the selection and upkeep of an instrument. You may have to point out your inadequacy concerning instruments before aid is forthcoming. Oddly enough, most teachers tend to be too lenient rather than too particular regarding the quality and adjustment of students' instruments. Continue to ask questions until the answers make sense so that you can base any judgements you make on reasonable grounds.

SIX

EVALUATING AND HANDLING EQUIPMENT

THE INSTRUMENT PARTS

As you become acquainted with your instrument you will find that it becomes easy to use the proper terms for its various parts once you know what they are. Students and parents will want to be familiar with the following items in particular:

BODY: Several woods are used in construction, maple for the back, spruce for the top, ebony for the hardwood appointments—pegs, fingerboard, tail piece, end pin, and sometimes the chinrest.

VARNISH: Many, many coats are required for the fine instruments. The colors vary from light blond, through the oranges and reds to deep browns. When handling an instrument, do so by supporting it by the neck and end pin as much as possible to avoid marring the varnish with the oils and acids of the hand.

SCROLL: Its function is to hold the pegs. All handmade instruments have individually carved scrolls which give them a unique characteristic.

PEGS: Each instrument has four, one assigned to each string. They should be made of ebony or rosewood and not a softer material painted black. They should be individually fitted into well aligned peg holes. When turning the pegs to adjust the tension of the string, they should not stick or bind but turn easily and stay where desired.

There are now several variations of "mechanical" pegs for violin, viola and cello which look almost like traditional pegs. These are constructed so that resistance to turning is not dependent upon friction of the peg against the peg box hole. Thus, they are not affected as much by weather conditions and always turn freely. They are particularly popular for school instruments and younger students.

String bases are equipped with mechanical metal screw-type pegs, which eliminate the need for string adjusters at the tail piece when chrome steel strings are used.

NECK: The neck should not be varnished between the scroll and the neck heel. It should feel very smooth, having been oiled and rubbed for ease of playing and to prevent stickiness between thumb and neck.

FINGERBOARD: This piece, usually of ebony, should be aligned along with the neck at the exact center of the instrument. It should be glued to the neck leaving no rough seams. Its top should be free from ridges to assure perfect response with the strings.

FINGERBOARD NUT: This important little piece of wood located at the top of the fingerboard plays a crucial part in the proper spacing and alignment of strings. If its grooves are too deep the strings will buzz against the fingerboard when played.

BRIDGE: Fitting a bridge to each individual instrument is extremely important. The feet must comply with the curve of the instrument top, and the top of the bridge has its shape determined by the end of the fingerboard. It is centered between the F-holes with the feet beside the F-hole notches.

Its thickness at the top is less than 1/16 of an inch, and its height is determined by specifications for the clearance of the strings above the fingerboard. You can see that it is a most particular piece!

Proper spacing of the string grooves on the bridge is important for playing ease. Watch that the grooves remain just deep enough to hold the strings in place. If more than ½ of the string becomes embedded in the top of the bridge, its tone is impaired.

SOUNDPOST: Another small but important piece, the soundpost, can be seen inside the instrument by sighting through the F-hole on the right side. It should appear just below the foot of the bridge and be perpendicular to the top and back.

CAUTION—The soundpost is not glued in. If string pressure is released from the bridge and thus from the top of the instrument, the soundpost may fall if the instrument is jarred slightly. It may have to be reset by a repairman. Conversely, if the instrument is bumped causing the soundpost to fall, the strings must all be loosened immediately. Their continued pressure could seriously damage the top of the instrument.

TAILPIECE: The position of the tailpiece is important for a well adjusted instrument. It is held by a tailgut to the end pin, and when properly in place the narrow end of the tailpiece is even with the ridge of the saddle. This assures a proper length of string between the wide end of the tailpiece and the bridge, and plenty of room for string adjusters.

STRING ADJUSTERS: These screw mechanisms which are located on or near the tailpiece affect the tension of the string either by direct pressure or by means of a lever. They enable the string to be tuned by very fine degrees. They are meant for use with chrome-steel strings or wire strings.

   If your instrument has wound gut-centered strings rather than steel-centered, fine-tuning string adjusters will be ineffective. They also may position the gut string so that its wrapping extends over the bridge in the playing area.

   At least one manufacturer makes the string adjuster part of the tailpiece. They are matching black and have a uniform appearance. However, if one misfunctions the whole tailpiece must be replaced.

ENDPIN: This rounded piece of ebony has the tailgut looped around it. It is not glued to the instrument, so if the tailpiece is removed the endpin could fall out. If the tailgut breaks releasing the tailpiece,all the strings, and the bridge, the instrument will seem to be a disaster area, and in your excitement the endpin may get lost.

CHINREST: This is not an intrinsic part of the violin, and can be exchanged for other models in a search for the most comfortable shape. Consult with your teacher if you suspect a chinrest poorly suited to the student.

SHOULDERPAD: This refers to a pad placed between the violin or viola and the player's shoulder area. It is usually attached to the instrument and removed after playing. They are controversial in that some teachers use them, some do not.

   There are many, many varieties of shoulder pads. Your selection of one could depend on what you think should be its function. Generally they should perform a dual function—to partially fill the space between jaw and body, and to secure the instrument in a comfortable playing position.

   For violins of half size or smaller, a rectangle of permanently soft vinyl or plastic sponge held with a rubber band will prove quite suitable. If your teacher has a preference, he will recommend a commercial brand. It is desireable to select a shoulder pad which is held by tension across the lower back of the violin and hooked over the edges of the bout, or one which is secured under the chinrest clamp. If the pad is of the type that slides around on the back of the instrument it could be a nuisance to control.

THE BOW

Pernambuco wood, the most desirable material for bows, is a type of Brazilwood which takes its name from the Brazilian state where it is found in abundance. It is very hard, stiff, heavy, strong, dense and non-porous with a fine, regular grain.

Lesser quality bows are usually made of ordinary Brazilwood or of fiberglass. Wood bows are susceptable to warping, fiberglass ones are not. Wood remains the undisputed material for bows in the minds of the professionals, but fiberglass bows are gaining in popularity for students, primarily because of their indestructability. They are also far less expensive.

By turning the bow screw button, the frog is pulled back, thus tightening the hair for playing. When this is done, the bow should show no signs of being warped from side to side when one sights down the top of the stick from frog to tip. When viewing the bow from the side, the stick should show retention of its arch, or dip, toward the hair even when it is tightened.

The hair of the bow is taken from Siberian horses, bleached white and processed. Hair for basses is frequently black or a mixture appearing gray. It is a coarser texture suitable for the heavier strings. Fiberglass bows usually have manufactured hair which is continuing to be scientifically developed and improved.

Mother-of-pearl, ivory, tortoise shell or other decorative material is frequently used for the frog slide and eye. The best bows have sterling silver or gold screw buttons and silver wrappings. The frog might be of a material other than ebony, such as ivory, and sometimes the artisan gives it a creative shape.

STRINGS

Good or better quality strings are necessary if the instrument is to respond with a tone equal to its potential. Your teacher might carry some strings with which to supply you, or make recommendations as to a good price range or a specific brand. The larger the instrument and the lower the string, the higher the price. A low E string on a bass could easily cost twenty times that of the high E string on a violin!

Types of Strings

There are several types of strings such as plain wire, wire wound with metal, plain gut and wound gut. Plain steel should be limited to the violin E string. Plain gut strings can occasionally be found on basses but have virtually become obsolete in favor of the developments in string manufacture over the past 25 years.

A beginning student's instrument should be equipped with steel strings which are wound with metal. These are the least affected by temperature and humidity and stay on the proper pitch for a longer period of time. They must be accompanied on the violin by four string adjusters at the tailpiece for ease of tuning.

Some student cellos have only the two highest sounding strings of wound steel, requiring two string adjusters.

If your instrument is ¾ or full size, your teacher might prefer wound gut strings, particularly for the two lower strings on the instrument. They have a more mellow sound. This type of string should be changed about every six months as opposed to once a year for the steel centered strings.

Basses will find two categories of strings, Orchestra Tuning and Solo Tuning. The latter are pitched one full tone higher, but you will probably never be concerned with these as a parent.

Small Size Strings

Small violins should be equipped with strings which are made for a specific size of instrument. Steel centered strings are available in sizes from 1/16 and 1/10 on up to full size 4/4. Do not try to make full size strings do for a 1/8 size violin, for instance.

ACCESSORIES

MUTES: To reduce, soften, or muffle the tone a mute is attached to or pressed against the bridge. Mutes come in a variety of shapes and designs. They are a necessity for the orchestra or ensemble player but few solos call for them.

In general, players prefer a design which allows the mute to be stored on the strings behind the bridge where it has no effect on the tone. It is then conveniently ready for use when needed.

A practice mute is a very heavy metal five-pronged device which subdues the tone so greatly that one should be able to practice in one room without disturbing someone in an adjacent area.

ROSIN: Each string player should have a cake of rosin in his case to apply to the bow before playing. It should be applied evenly and not too heavily since that would cause a gritty tone.

Rosin is available in light and dark shades, and several packaging styles. Until a student becomes advanced, he would do well to have his rosin encased in a wood trough since it is brittle and breaks easily. The experienced player usually prefers a dark rosin shaped a little larger than a marshmallow and glued to a square of felt which wraps around it to serve as a case.

IDENTIFICATION: Cases, violins and especially bows can become hopelessly confused as to ownership during gatherings of several hundred Suzuki violin students attending a Festival, or at an all-city orchestra meeting. As soon as you acquire your instrument outfit, see that it can be quickly and easily identified.

Cases can have luggage labels or colored yarn attached to the handle in addition to your name and address on paper inside the case. Plastic tape with the letters embossed is attractive, inside and outside of the case, but it tends to peel off after awhile.

Identifying the violin is a little more difficult. First, examine the instrument so you can remember unique marks or features such as scratches or mis-matched pegs. In addition, the elementary age student should have a tiny piece of colored yarn or string for identification tied somewhere on the instrument, perhaps on a peg, endpin, or section of the string which falls between the bridge and tailpiece. Or place a very small set of initials in pencil on the bridge.

Bows can also carry a small piece of yarn or colored tape around the stick near the frog, or put your name or initials on masking tape or plastic tape and attach to the side of the frog which is held facing the player.

CASES

Because it is the case that is most visable to the public, it is understandable that your child might balk at carrying a very old and battered case which has had decades of use. More important, that old case might not be doing the job it should in protecting the instrument and bow.

As with most other large items under discussion, cases range from very reasonable to very expensive. Although high cost may bring you built-in luxury in features and materials, a moderately priced case can furnish you with ample convenience and protection.

Violins and Violas

Cases for violins come in two basic forms—oblong and shaped. The oblong ones are rectangular. The shaped ones are the familiar kind that almost look like a violin. The oblong ones provide more space for accessories, but the protection offered by either one depends on its quality and interior fittings.

A violin or viola case should be of sturdy hard material. The exterior might be vinyl, canvas, leather or paper resembling grained leather. It should have two or three fasteners which can be operated easily by children's fingers. The top should close and seal without forcing, causing no doubt as to whether or not the contents are being "squeezed" to get it shut.

Inside, the instrument should fit snugly without having to be forced down. Neither should there be excess space surrounding it which would permit it to shift around within the case.

The violin can be kept safe from damage by loose objects in the case, including small bits of rosin, if it is wrapped in a soft cloth before being placed in the case. One might use flannel, an old pillow case, a silk head scarf or a satin bag which fits over the whole violin.

A French fitted case means the scroll as well as the body of the violin lies in an area particularly shaped for it. This is slightly more protective but not a necessity.

The lining can be simple or elegant, made of felt or flannel or more luxurious heavy velvet plush in radiant colors. Extra padding around the sides and on the bottom of the case is desirable. A compartment with a cover is needed to hold rosin for the bow and other small accessories needed, such as a mute, tuning fork, pitch pipe, packaged strings, pencil for orchestra, chinrest key for tightening, and even a fingernail clipper.

If your child uses a shoulder pad it is convenient to have a case which provides interior space for it. This could be in the closed compartment or simply beside the scroll or neck where it does not interfere with the case closing. If this is not possible, parents make a small drawstring bag to hold the shoulder pad which attaches to the case's handle.

Student model instruments frequently come in Thermoplastic molded cases. They are attractive and durable but may need additional padding inside. Some models have provisions for a carrying strap on the outside—ideal for students who have to ride bike or bus and carry books in addition.

Be sure your case has a secure place for one or more bows. The bow should not work loose from the bow clips while being transported as it might damage the violin.

CAUTION: Although keys are usually furnished with new student cases, do *not* lock the case. In fact, the key should probably be removed and stored in a jewelry box, or your child might arrive at a lesson with his instrument securely stored in a case for which he cannot find the key!

Cellos and Basses

Cello and bass cases for daily student use have traditionally been soft canvas lined with flannel and reinforced with vinyl or leather at stress points. New materials are now available which are expanding the choices to include thicker more protective cases that are also light weight.

For the cellist who transports his instrument frequently, either locally or cross-country, a hard shell case is a necessity. Naturally, they are awkward to carry, but again the materials being developed are creating lightweight sleek cases with frequent improvements being introduced. Be certain that the case fits your cello properly for maximum protection.

Hard cases for basses are found primarily among symphony musicians and the like who entrust the transportation of their instrument to stage crews. Heavy, well padded flexible vinyl cases provide protection during normal travel and personal handling.

MUSIC STANDS

An essential piece of equipment for the child who is beginning to read music on a string instrument is a good quality music stand. Poor posture and fatigue can often be attributed to the manner in which the student must read from his music.

Although cellists sit down to play, the violinist, violist and bassist frequently stand. This means that you might as well select a stand at the beginning which will satisfy the height requirements of your child right into adulthood.

There are basically two types of music stands, folding or portable, and studio models. Your student may eventually play in a small ensemble for which he will need a folding stand, so selecting a good quality stand of this description could be a long-range investment. They are much less expensive than the studio models but also less sturdy, making it difficult to write on the music or support several books.

Studio models are non-portable, should have a solid smooth back and be adjustable to suit your height requirements. Schools use durable models which could be recommended by your teacher. Music stores can order more elegant wooden models to enhance your home music room or living room.

SEVEN

INSPIRATION, MOTIVATION, APPLICATION

Everything that touches your child's world leaves him with an impression. Parents frequently make comments to the effect that they did not think a child noticed something, only to discover later that it made a lasting impression.

At some time in your youngster's life he will form his opinion about string instruments. Since parents get first chance at shaping their children's attitudes, it is hoped that from the day of birth their home would be filled with fine music and the rich sounds of orchestral and solo strings. Growing up in this type of environment has resulted in many of history's great musicians.

But perhaps your child's introduction to string instruments has come from outside the home. Or perhaps you as a family have recently developed an interest in this aspect of music. Your motivation is now strong and you eagerly anticipate the future when your own home-grown version of "Orange Blossom Special" or "Joy To The World" will be heard from the living room.

ENCOURAGE THE DESIRE TO LEARN

Hearing exciting music on television, at school, by a friend, or at a concert, will immediately stimulate some children to become involved and to try it for themselves. Others will be more complacent, not because they dislike string music but because they are concerned about the reactions of others. Will they be made fun of? Will they fail?

If you want your child involved in musical training through the medium of string instruments, be encouraging and enthusiastic from the first day that the topic comes up. Lead him to think there is no question that he will be successful. Talk about people you know who play instruments and enjoy it. What fun it will be to learn melodies and play with friends.

A teacher can lead children to be aware of their own shortcomings by an amusing but direct comment, as does Harry Kobialka of Potsdam, N.Y.

Be realistic, too. Observe that performers make it look so easy, but you are sure they have worked very hard to make it sound so nice. Point out that the language of music is like other languages—you begin like a child learning sounds and words before being able to speak sentences and tell stories.

Keeping up your enthusiasm may become difficult once you are subjected to the daily routine of practice, but it is absolutely essential. Your attitude, combined with the environment you create at home, will play a significant part in sustaining your child's interest.

Motivation

What is it that motivates a person to achieve in music? There are many answers, depending on the individual, but there are certain things that parents and teachers can control to stimulate the desire to learn:

1) **Make music a valuable part of your life, worthy of time and effort, and your children will have an example to follow.**

Musical activity in the family seems to be a major factor in a student's desire to play an instrument and, more important, indications are that it is also linked to the amount of success realized.

Family involvement of a positive nature can be observed in the Suzuki approach where it is necessary for a parent to attend lessons and direct practice because of the age of the student. Very young children are anxious to please their parents and the Suzuki philosophy has proven tremendously successful in capitalizing on this fact.

A doctoral study by George William Robinson at Texas Technological University found that among older children encouragement by the father is a particularly positive factor. Also, a student's belief that an older sibling is eager for him to learn is a strong asset.

If your family attends concerts, enjoys the sound of good music in the home, and admires those who play musical instruments well, your children will probably place a high value on music.

2) **Help your child build skills and confidence through regular practice and good instruction.**

The adage "Nothing succeeds like success" is applicable here, and the student who plays daily and works systematically on the assigned task can easily see how far he has come in a short period of time. One day away from a string instrument can make it seem like a stranger. The psychological effects are immediately noticeable in the player's lack of security and pleasure.

3) **Acknowledge your child's achievement with compliments, encouragement and above all, your whole-hearted support for his musical activities.**

A music teacher said that to him the most heartbreaking scene is that of a parent dropping a child off in front of the building on the evening of the school music department's concert and telling him to phone for a ride home when he's finished playing. Disinterest on the part of a parent will show up soon in the child's attitude and directly affect his success.

Encouragement and earned compliments can help the discouraged student through periods of depression. Even when things are going normally, a tremedous lift is felt when a parent says something like "That new piece sounds better every day" or, "Your tone is so much fuller this week".

4) **Encourage participation in group sessions, orchestra, other musical organizations, and concert attendance with peers.**

For young people, the influence of the group is very strong. Small children enjoy watching and learning from others. Older children like to feel that they are not alone in their interest and difficulties, and the teen-ager derives much fulfillment in being with friends of mutual interests and abilities.

Students who belong to performing groups participate in special activities which give them a sense of satisfaction as well as belonging. The motivation to efficiently complete academic work in order to be eligible for a special music trip or contest has improved many children's approach to homework assignments.

5) **Encourage music performance in your home and with friends.**
One of the great advantages of string instruments is that they are perfectly suited for music in the home in groups of two, three, four or more. There is a long heritage of literature from which to draw. Present-day arrangers have collected and frequently simplified many duets and other chamber music (a term given to music designed for intimate surroundings). Also being met are the demands for popular, rock, country and show tunes by arranging them for solo and instrumental combinations.

From the Parent

Although there should be a concerned parent behind every child, the purpose of all education is to make that child a responsible and functioning adult. Participation in musical activities offers a wealth of opportunities to grow in maturity. The student should be encouraged to accept the responsibility and challenges of his musical activity, but until he becomes familiar with what is expected of him, the parent should remain alert to see that the jobs are getting done.

Much depends on the age of the child when it comes to accepting responsibility. Every student, however, is old enough to take care of his instrument insofar as carrying it and learning to handle it. Tiny children may need help in tightening the bow hair, but even a three-year-old can put on a shoulder sponge or pull out a cello endpin.

Emphasize to the older student the importance of remembering the lesson day and time. Some students easily "forget" their lesson, especially if it is unprepared!

Establish from the beginning that it is not acceptable to be late to lessons—even if the teacher appears to be busy when you arrive. If the responsibility for transportation is yours, be sure your activities do not result in tardiness to lessons or the need for complicated rearrangements on a regular basis. If the child is to get to his lessons on his own, check for a reasonable period of time that he does so.

At least once a semester have a conversation with your child's teacher. However, never discuss the child's problems in his presence. If you are worried about how he practices or reacts to his music in other ways, speak with the teacher in private. The teacher will be pleased that you want to talk with him about the problem.

Scheduling Other Activities

Assuming that you wish to act as a guide to your children in helping them select activities to go along with music, there are four considerations to keep in mind:

1) Every child should have some free time with no commitment during which he can follow his interest of that particular moment.
2) Some activities require considerable dicipline and quality work which means preparation between sessions (like music lessons).
3) Some activities are strictly for fun with little if any demand for preparation in between time.
4) In requesting activities, children are influenced by their peers, and parents should evaluate an activity on its real worth to the child, make their decisions, and stick with it.

Generally speaking, a child can succesfully participate in two or three activities, depending on the preparation needed. If one of the activities needs outside preparation (such as a private music lesson) one or two others "just for fun" would be sufficient, remembering the need for some "free time". Our modern society tends to push for involvement in as much as possible, but the child who can do something on a quality level is frequently the most happy with himself and consequently with his life in general.

PRACTICE

Certainly the question most frequently asked of a teacher has to do with the amount of time a child should practice. Age, advancement, length of concentration, motivation and goals are but a few of the things which influence the answer.

For example, the seven-year-old who has just begun violin may be doing well with five minutes at a time, but this should be done two or three times a day. Another seven-year-old who started when he was three might be playing concerto movements by now and quite joyfully putting in two hours a day. An older beginner in upper elementary school or beyond might be so highly motivated that he spends every available minute working with the instrument. A more typical example would be a student who has been given a specific assignment, been told what material is to be covered, and the amount of time each day he should spend working at it. Whatever the situation, your teacher should give you an idea of how much time is expected of your child for his particular level.

How practice time is spent is extremely important. A general outline of what is to be covered will be suggested by the teacher and it will depend on the method or system being used. But the most significant element in practice will be your child's determination to achieve the goals which have been set. This will help to decide the *quality* of his practice.

One of the teacher's most important jobs is to teach the student *how* to practice. If a lesson consisted of nothing else but how to work out several difficult passages during the week, it would be a good session.

Children must be taught what to listen for when they practice. Otherwise, it seems most of them would be content to simply get the right fingers down and play as fast as possible! All the "right" fingers will do little good unless they are in exactly the place where they sound correct, or "in tune". This means time must be taken to hear each note, which requires a certain amount of slow careful practice.

Because of the intricate movement of the left, or fingering, hand, many students underestimate the important roll of the right arm which, through the bow, produces the basic tone, texture, dynamics (loud and soft) and character of the music. Practice which helps the student isolate the problems of the bow and solve them will sound strange to the listener. However, this is also a very important part of practice.

Setting a Time

The hour of the day or evening that a student does his practice can have much to do with his rate of progress. Practice before the school day begins is very profitable, although difficult to get established. It leaves room for a shorter, more relaxed session later in the afternoon if desired.

Work out a practice schedule with your child, remembering to consider some free time immediately after school along with the general pattern of his friends activities. Give the chosen time a week's trial. When it is finally agreed to, be firm about adhering to it. Do not forget to schedule something for Saturday and Sunday, which could be more productive than crowded weekdays.

When motivation to practice is hard to come by, try one or more of the following suggestions:
1) Keep a practice record of time spent. Earn a new record album for every 1000 or 2500 minutes. Choosing the recording will be educational—as well as the adding!
2) Make a list of seven specific things to be done during practice including how many times or how long each should be worked on. Check off as done. (This is designed to improve skills through plain repetition which frequently leads to improved attitude.) Practice is over when the list has been completed.

3) Change the location or setting of the practice area. Make a pleasant music corner complete with pictures, music file, stand, lamp, etc.
4) Have your teacher record on cassette tape some selections to be practiced. Alternate listening and playing with the tape.
5) Tape record the same piece after practice every day for a week and observe the improvement at the end of the week.
6) Pick out a book of pieces at the music store containing some familiar pop tunes, Christmas songs or show pieces. Even if they are too difficult, the student will re-discover them next year and recognize his progress.
7) Set a realistic goal for memorizing a given number of measures a day. Try to get ahead of your goal.
8) Invite a friend to come in on a certain day next week. Prepare for this event.

Summertime

Beware of vacations! If they are long enough (such as all summer), and badly handled (such as no music at all), you can lose practically a school year's progress. Perhaps much of the ability will return in a short time, but the work is hard and without much joy.

Schedule practice into the summer hours just as you did during the school year. If your teacher is available, continue your study. If not, create a program of daily review and ask your teacher for recommendations.

When your child reaches a sufficient proficiency level he will be eligible for a camp experience with a concentrated music emphasis. These usually run from one to eight weeks in length. Be sure to get your teacher's recommendation on what is available since one may be more suitable for your child at his particular age and level than another.

Children enrolled in a Suzuki program can attend what is called a summer Institute even before they learn to play! Since a parent is involved, these Institutes frequently attract the entire family for a week at a time. Pre-schoolers through teen-agers attend two to six hours a day of class and engage in other typical summer activities when not busy at their favorite sport of music making.

EIGHT

TO SIT OR TO STAND

For violin or viola students, whether to sit or stand while practicing should be discussed with the teacher. Some teachers will be relatively unconcerned about the subject. Other feel strongly about it.

Students in the Suzuki method will have no choice in the matter. All of their activities are done standing and by memory until they reach a relatively advanced playing stage.

It is when the student needs to refer to the notes that he assumes a relatively stationary location, and it seems normal and logical to sit.

Then why the question?

Sitting in front of a music stand is frequently approached like sitting at a desk or the dinner table, where your attention is directed to what is in front of you. This is quite acceptable for cellists and clarinetists since their playing is also happening right in front. The young violinists will almost instinctively sit squarely in front of the music and allow the violin to creep forward and downward altering the desired posture to the extent that poor habits could be established.

To counteract this, the teacher must give specific instructions about how to play while seated which can be followed at home with a little help from a parent. These directions may depend on the teacher's concept of acceptable posture. Almost certainly it would involve sitting on the front half of the chair with both feet touching the floor.

Other recommendations might be:
1) Place the stand about two feet from the front of the chair.
2) Either turn the chair slightly to the right or move the stand to the left. This is to encourage having a view of the bow on the strings, the fingers, and music all in one direction. Do not twist the torso.

- 43 -

3) Have the bottom of the music rack close to scroll level.
4) Light on the music should be equal to or better than that which is needed for ordinary reading.
5) Lower the right knee a little to accomodate the bow hand when playing on the first, or highest pitched string.

It is not to be implied that a standing posture will eliminate the problems often caused by sitting. However, standing for realistic periods of time has some intrinsic attributes:

1) One tends to stand with a straight back, since it is actually hard work to stand and play slouched.
2) Balance can be shifted from one foot to the other giving alternate relaxation to certain muscles.
3) Memory of note groups or phrases can be encouraged since the student is free to turn from the music or "wander" about the room while testing his ability.
4) An unnatural twisting of the body is less likely, and the bow will be unhampered in its movement by the knees.

For some students, an assignment which specifies whether to sit or stand while working on a given selection could increase the enjoyment and novelty of practice.

NINE

USE OF RECORDS AND CASSETTE TAPES

There are basically three ways to use records and tapes. Each is aimed at speeding up the learning process and improving it.

1) Listening to fine quality music, particularly performances featuring the instrument to be studied.
2) Using cassette tapes of the material to be learned, which is presented in an educational format for daily home study.
3) Recording oneself in order to analyze the performance for improvement possibilities.

Performance Recordings

To know where one is going is essential in any human undertaking. Asking a student to practice on an instrument without having heard that instrument in solo performance by a professional, or even having heard it in its finest orchestral rolls, is like trying to draw a picture of something without having seen it.

The more a student hears good quality music played by recognized performers, the better will be his idea of the goal. True, he may never come close in his mastery of the instrument, but he will be learning the language of music as pronounced by the most eloquent spokesmen of the art, and his ideals will be raised above the initial utterings of his inept bow arm.

Also, the importance of fine music in the home as displayed by parents in their devotion to quality music will set the stage for the priority that the child gives to music. Children are little affected by lip service; they are silently but deeply influenced by what kind of music plays an important part in the lives of their parents.

Cassette Learning Tapes

In recent years we have come to fuller realization of the part that recorded material can play in speeding up the learning process. From early infancy the baby learns an incredible amount through his ears. Since music is an aural art, it follows that much about learning how to make music can be acquired through listening.

This concept is the foundation of the Suzuki philosophy as well as the cornerstone of several teaching methods now on the market. But it need not be limited to students of selected methods. If a teacher is in agreement as to its benefits, he can make tape recordings of things to be worked on at home. This individualized instruction can give attention to setting the speed for practice, isolating the difficult passages and giving the correct image of the rhythm and intonation to prevent erroneous learning which requires extensive remedial work.

Criticisms of this type of learning do exist, but they seem to lack substantiation. Some fear that they prevent a student from having to work out everything for himself. However, a "practice tape" is simply a lesson at home every day, and it helps assure correct images from the beginning.

Self-Recording

Anyone who has ever recorded his voice or rendition of a musical selection will attest to the shock it can produce upon hearing it played back! At what point the student is ready to experience this trauma must be decided by parent and teacher, but painful as it may be, much can be gained from the child recording his best piece and then listening to it with a critical ear.

A new tape recorder is little more than a toy at first, but after the novelty has passed it can be a most effective self-teacher.

TEN

WHEN THE INSTRUMENT IS NOT IN USE

Children (even adults) are eager to return to other activities after their practice, so it should be established from the beginning that a few seconds must be taken to return the instrument and bow to the case. Time must be allowed to loosen the tension on the bow hair, remove the shoulder pad on violin and viola, return the endpin into the cello or bass, and make certain the case has been fastened.

CAUTION: Never put the violin into the case and shut the lid without securely closing the fasteners. Somehow we assume that a case is sealed tightly if the lid is down, and many instruments have hit the floor when the case is picked up and the top falls open.

Protect the instrument from temperature extremes. At home do not store the case beside the heat source or in the sunlight of a window.

An instrument left in the car during the summer will be more protected in the trunk than in the interior, where the sun beating on the glass creates an oven-like heat.

Although a good case offers some insulation, rather than store an instrument all day in an automobile it is still advisable to take it indoors. You may have to keep the instrument for your child while you are at work so that it might be convenient for him to pick up after school for a lesson or rehearsal. If the instrument has gotten extremely hot or cold in the car, it could take the duration of the lesson for it to recover its normal temperature and stay in tune!

During practice, if the violin is laid down, put it on a table or a place higher and larger than a chair.

If a cello or bass is left outside of its case and laid on its side in a safe area, put the endpin *into* the instrument. It is very likely otherwise, to catch some unsuspecting leg!

Basses can be stood in an unoccupied corner of the room rather safely. Lean the bass slightly toward the corner with the bridge facing the corner. The lower bouts will touch each side wall to support the instrument. The bass bow can be slipped under the E string which will hold it firmly against the fingerboard with the point close to the bridge. Some players store the bow in this manner even when the bass is in its case.

ELEVEN

CARE AND MAINTENANCE OF STRING INSTRUMENTS

In admiring your newly acquired instrument one of your first thoughts should be, "I'm going to take especially good care of this." With a few simple instructions, you can keep your instrument and bow looking their best.

However, if you are typical, you will also think how complex it must be to learn to handle and adjust it without making some grievous error. Like any precision tool, your instrument must be in adjustment to function properly, and by following a few guidelines and getting some firsthand help from your teacher, you will be able to keep it in good playing condition and also spot trouble areas that need an expert's hand.

THE CASE

Even the very young student should share in the pride of ownership and care of the string instrument. The simplist instructions should not be omitted, such as how to carry the case and remove the instrument.

Swinging the case in free air obviously will not damage the instrument, but young fingers do slip and obstructions do interfere seemingly from out of nowhere. A strong jolt to the case, even with the instrument well protected inside, could knock down the sound post or jar loose the bridge, and more complex damage could follow.

When carrying the cello case, hold it with the bridge toward your body. Going through doors, position the cello in front of you so you can watch to protect it, even if you have to back through the opening!

Removing from the Case

The seasoned player observes in disbelief the awkward ways that the new student can find to open his case and remove the instrument! Included in the first lesson should be a step by step demonstration on how to take out the instrument and prepare it for playing.

THE INSTRUMENT

Violin and Viola

Before opening the violin or viola case, lay it securely on a flat surface which will support the entire case. Be sure it is right side up with the handle and clips facing you. Open the lid slowly in case a dislodged bow might be caught on the instrument. Lift out only the instrument, grasping it by the neck. Attach the shoulder pad if one is to be used.

Lay the violin down in the case while removing the bow. Release the frog end of the bow from its clip, pull it out from the case an inch or so, and then slide the tip or point of the bow out of its holder. The beginner's first tendency is to take the frog end and pull it toward him, forgetting to safely slide the tip free. Odds are equal as to which breaks first, the bow tip or the holder on the case!

After tightening the bow hair and putting rosin on it, lift out the instrument again and shut the lid. This will protect any contents of the case and also insure the continued alignment of the case with its lid which may tend to twist if allowed to stand upright while open.

Cello and Bass

Most cellists and bassists will have soft or canvas cases. The instruments are awkward to handle for a beginner, and a demonstration on how to safely and expediently separate the instrument and its case should be given by the teacher.

Remove the bow first and lay it in a safe place. Without laying the instrument down, undo the fasteners (zipper or snaps) and work the case upward on the instrument. Slip your hand up under the case and *firmly* grasp the instrument's neck, holding it solidly while the case is removed.

Before replacing the bag, turn the zippers outward away from the interior of the case to prevent them from scratching the instrument while the case is being put on. The case will fall into place over a cello, and the instrument can be turned upside down and rested lightly on its scroll while you complete the fastening.

If you have snap fasteners, be extremely cautious about the pressure you use to close them. Be alert to spot any damage from roughness inside the case such as might be caused by unprotected zipper teeth.

MAINTENANCE THAT YOU CAN DO

Keep it Clean

Keep the finish on the body of your instrument clean by wiping it after every use. Use a flannel cloth or an old piece of fabric which has become very soft. Keep the wiping cloth in your case.

Occasionally treat the body (the varnished areas) with a cleaning polish made especially for orchestral string instruments, which can be obtained from your dealer. It will safely remove stubborn rosin collections under the bowing area of the strings, and polish out fingerprints.

CAUTION: Do *not* use polish on any area except the varnished body and scroll. Avoid the neck, fingerboard, strings, chinrest and the like.

Do *not* use a household furniture polish unless it has been approved by your violinmaker or teacher.

Do *not* carry the polish in your case.

Vacuum the violin case periodically to remove particles of rosin and other dirt.

Cleaning the Strings

Day to day wiping of the fingerboard and strings is the best maintenance. An accumulation of rosin on the strings in the playing area may eventually require special attention. A small amount of alcohol on a cloth can be rubbed the length of the string without harm to the ebony fingerboard, and it will loosen the soil and rosin. *Extreme care* must be taken to keep the alcohol from touching any varnished part of the instrument. It is recommended that you cover the top of the instrument with a cloth while using alcohol to clean the string. Stubborn collections of rosin can also be removed from the string's playing area by gently using "Triple O" steel wool.

Where to Keep the Instrument

Store your instrument in its case where it is not subjected to extremes of temperature. Keep it away from heating and cooling vents, and be sure it is not in the sunlight through a window.

The strings are to be kept tight, or "in tune", when the instrument is stored. They should not be loosened as is the bow hair.

If you must be away, such as on vacation, place the case in a room where the temperature and humidity will not change radically.

Pegs: Slipping and Sticking

Temperature, humidity and wear affect the performance of the pegs. They may become hard, almost impossible, to turn, making fine adjustment difficult. Or you may find them easy to adjust only to find they will not stay where they should.

Good pegs, those of ebony or rosewood in particular, should function with little trouble if they have been fitted well initially.

If the pegs are of the mechanical type with the screw in the end, the adjustment is purely a mechanical one. The screw can be tightened or loosened so the pegs will function easily yet stay in place.

For wood pegs that do not hold their place, apply ordinary white chalk. This can probably be done without completely removing the string. Loosen the string until only one revolution is around the peg. Pull the peg out slightly until you can apply the chalk to the affected area.

When the pegs seem to freeze in the holes, a mild lubricant is called for. Several substances might be used, but very sparingly, or too much will create the opposite problem. A soft lead (graphite) pencil makes a good start. Soap is another material. There are also commercial lubricants, produced by string instrument manufacturers, whose sole purpose is to keep strings from "sticking".

Nothing you do will make the seriously worn peg trouble free. If, after you have had some experience with tuning instruments, you suspect the pegs themselves are at fault, get your teacher's appraisal of the problem or go directly to the violinmaker to whom this is a common occurrence.

String Adjusters or Screw Tuners

Tuners which adjust the string tension by a lever action can be silent damaging culprits. As the screw depresses the lever, it could come in contact with the varnish and wood under the tailpiece, causing a bad bruise before even being suspected. Therefore, check almost daily that this is not in danger of happening. To raise the lever away from the top, turn the screw to the left and raise the pitch of the string by using the peg.

If the string adjuster seems to have no effect, the screw might be stripped. This means the complete unit must be replaced. It is not a difficult procedure and can be done in a few minutes by you, your teacher or the store from whom you purchase a new one. If you would like to match the adjuster to others on the instrument, take the instrument with you.

The Bridge

If the bridge is not properly fitted and adjusted, many aspects of playing are affected. Check the following features:
1) If the two outside strings are not equidistant from the edges of the fingerboard, the bridge has been moved sideways.
2) The bridge should be positioned between the inner notches on the F-holes.
3) The side of the bridge near the tailpiece should be perpendicular to the top of the instrument.
4) The grooves which carry the strings should allow at least ½ of the string to rest above the bridge for a resonant sound.
5) The feet should be shaped to fit the contour of the top of the instrument and they should be quite thin.
6) The bridge should not appear to be warped (arched or bent) from either side view or a top view.

To correct the above items, do the following:
Item 1: To move the bridge sideways, grasp the bridge firmly between thumb and forefinger with both hands, brace the instrument and slide the bridge horizontally into line. check strings for alignment. Prevent reoccurrence by handling violins gently when they are at "rest position" under the right arm. If trouble persists, have teacher or repairman coat the bridge feet with powdered rosin to help it "stick".
CAUTION: Do *not* glue the bridge to the instrument.

Item 2: Grasp bridge firmly as above. If bridge is reluctant to slide to the correct position between the notches, loosen the strings slightly. Do not jar the instrument or the soundpost may fall. Position the bridge so it leans slightly toward the tailpiece, and as you tighten the strings with the pegs the bridge will be pulled into a more perpendicular line.
Item 3: When strings are tuned they tend to pull the bridge forward toward the pegs. Grasp the top of the bridge between the strings or at the upper corners and gently force the bridge into a perpendicular position.
Items 4, 5 and 6: These conditions can be dealt with best by a repairman. Let you teacher assess the seriousness of the problem if you have doubts.

THE BOW

Things That You Can Do

The essentials of daily care for the bow can effectively be presented in a series of DOs and DON'Ts:

DO handle the bow with care; it is almost as fragile as it looks.

DO release the tension on the hair when it is not in use by turning the screw counter-clockwise several times.

DO apply a good grade of rosin sparingly on the entire length of the bow before each use. Basses stroke the rosin from frog to tip only.

DO wipe the stick with a soft cloth before putting it away.

DO NOT let the student swing, wave or whip the bow in the air.

DO NOT tighten the bow hair to the extent that the stick looses its inward curve toward the hair.

DO NOT touch the bow hair, particularly with fingers, clothing, hair and other skin surfaces.

DO NOT use polish on the stick of the bow.

Although delicate, the bow is a generally reliable piece of equipment. Its simplist and most frequent problem is a broken hair, or a hair which sags away from the others. You should deal with this by using a scissors and cutting the hair off close to each end. The professional player often breaks off the broken hair by pulling it away in the opposite direction from the rest of the hair, but it is a calculated risk that the whole shank will be pulled loose in an avalanche of hair! Recommendation: Cut, do not pull.

Things For Your Repairman To Do

The hair of the bow must periodically be replaced. This is known as rehairing. When the hair becomes smooth and has difficulty making the strings vibrate well, the violinmaker can put in new horsehair or one of the continually developing synthetics.

Students are known to wait until only a few hairs remain in the bow before rehairing! A policy of beginning each school year with fresh hair should be established. Although the amount of playing determines wear on the hair, it is age that makes the hair brittle, causing excess breaking and thinning.

The screw passes through an eyelet which is attached to the frog, and either one of these can become worn. They can be replaced by a repairman.

Wooden bows, particularly those in the lower price range, tend to warp. This can be observed by sighting down the top of the bow from frog to tip when the bow is tightened. Any warping is undesirable, but a mild case can be tolerated and even remedied by the violinmaker.

The Dirty Bow

Care of the bow should begin the day it is acquired. When a student points out that his bow hair has become gray and shiny, and the frog area is caked with a black unknown, it is a sign of carelessness. A rehairing job is usually the solution although the question continues to arise, "Can I wash the hair of my bow?"

Stories involving this action are so varied that it is difficult to give counsel with conviction. Horsehair stretches when wet and could dry unevenly. If you have a nice wooden bow and the hair seem terribly soiled, it is probably time to have it rehaired and not take the risks that a soap and water job entail.

If you have a fiberglass bow with one of the synthetic hairs, and find that it has become soiled even though your student has not worn it out by practicing, you could try removing some of the soil with a cleanser and tooth brush and water.

HOW TO CHANGE A STRING

Although changing a string is not complicated, it is much easier if you have watched it being done.

Replacements for each string should be carried in the case at all times. If the strings you use are the chrome-steel variety you can carry a full set of new ones since they do not deteriorate. If some of your strings are metal wound on gut, you should keep an old string as a temporary replacement in case the present one breaks, and buy a fresh one at your dealers as soon as possible. The gut center strings do become old and more brittle if stored by players for long periods.

Procedure

1) Remove the old string from the peg and the tailpiece. Do NOT loosen or change more than one string at a time so that tension might be kept on the bridge. Also, the pegs will not get mixed up.
2) Insert the loop end of the new string into the tailpiece hole or attach it to the string adjuster in the same manner as the old string.
3) Thread the straight end of the string through the hole in the proper peg until it shows through about ¼ inch or more.

4) Wind the peg away from you, keeping the string taut, and crossing it back over itself for security.
5) As all the slack is taken up, be sure the string is positioned in its groove on the bridge and on the fingerboard nut. If there is a bridge protector on the string, place it in position between the bridge and the string.
6) Between the nut and the peg, the string should continue in a straight line as illustrated.
7) Tune the string slowly bringing it to pitch. A metal wound gut string will continue to stretch for hours, sometimes longer. A steel string will hold its pitch almost from the start. CAUTION: Be sure that you have string adjusters at the tailpiece for the steel wound strings. If you are using metal wound *gut* strings (the little loop at the end is obviously *not* metal) be sure to remove the string adjuster. Not only is the adjuster relatively ineffective, but the gut string attached to it will be positioned incorrectly, often with the wrapping extending over the bridge into the playing area.

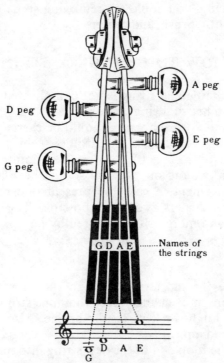

Photo© 1961 Neil A. Kjos Music Co., used in Muller-Rusch String Method for Violin, Book One. Reprinted with permission.

TWELVE

TUNING

Unless each string on the instrument sounds exactly like the pitch or sound which it is supposed to represent, the player will find that putting his finger in the assigned location on the fingerboard will not produce the sound he is after. One of two things happens: he persists in keeping his finger in the same spot, thus sounding very "sour", or he slides his finger to the sound which he wants, meaning he is not acquiring the automatic feel for where each pitch is located and probably will never play without sliding into tones.

Tuning the instrument properly before playing, and occasionally during a playing period if you suspect a change, is absolutely essential. Doing this successfully requires practice and probably some help at the beginning.

Begin by understanding how the pegs and string adjusters affect the sound of the strings. When adjusters at the tailpiece are screwed in, they tighten the string and make it sound higher. When the pegs in the scroll are turned away from you, they wind the string tighter and thus higher.

Tuning the string means comparing it to something and adjusting it to sound the same. Usually a string player uses a piano, pitch pipe or tuning fork at home, which is tuned to the note A equaling 440 vibrations per second. Once the A is in tune, the other strings are tuned by comparing the E and/or D to the A, and then the remaining strings to an already tuned one (D compared to A, G compared to D, C compared to G).

With all the instruments, truly accurate tuning can be done only while bowing the strings. On all but bass, two strings are played simultaneously and adjusted while being sounded. This takes considerable dexterity, and until you or your child develop it, the "plucking" method can be used.

Procedure

1) Sound A on the piano (or pitch pipe or tuning fork) while holding the instrument facing you.

   Listen carefully to the tone while it finishes ringing before you pluck the A string.

   Decide whether your string should be made higher or lower to match the sound. If you cannot tell, assume that it is slightly low and proceed to adjust it to be higher.

   WITH PEGS: Grasp the A peg between thumb and index finger of right hand and turn it as though *un*screwing it slightly. The A will then probably be too low, so with a slow twisting motion "screw" in the peg, testing the string by thumb plucking as you go. The peg should stick as you reach the correct sound.

   If you get too high or not high enough, repeat the process. You may need to do this several times. Guard against a sound which may be too low.

   WITH STRING ADJUSTERS: Screw in the adjuster on the A string, (start with about a ¼ turn) and compare the two tones again.

   Continue to alternate the tones and turn the adjuster screw until the sounds seem to match.

   You may pass the matching point and have to reverse the direction of the adjuster on the violin.

2) Tune the D string next. On all but the bass, the strings are five tones apart, or in musical terms a "fifth". You can locate the pitch in your mind or with your voice by thinking of the first notes of the *Star Spangled Banner* - "Oh - oo - say . . ." The first "Oh" is the A, and "say" is the D string sound.

   Continue to hum the desired pitch as you turn the adjuster, returning frequently to the higher string for comparison.

   As a beginner to tuning, you may wish to sound D on the piano or pitch pipe, but soon you should learn to compare D to the A string for tuning.

3) Tune the G by singing down from D on the *Star Spangled Banner*.

4) Tune the E by singing or playing up five notes. The first two tones of *Twinkle, Twinkle Little Star* are a "fifth" apart, so by plucking the A string two times for the first "Twin-kle" you can hear in your mind what the next "Twinkle" should sound like. Or you might sing up a five-note scale.

CELLO: Follow the same general procedure as for violin.

Cello pegs will be gripped by the full hand and may require considerable strength to adjust.

Chrome-steel strings for A and D accompanied by string adjusters help the beginning student to tune easily.

BASS: Strings will be sounded individually for tuning, at first comparing them to a piano or other instrument. The more advanced player will use natural harmonics when tuning to bring the sound into a higher register where tones are more easy to compare. His teacher will explain harmonics and the technic used in tuning.

THIRTEEN

TROUBLESHOOTING

"My violin sounds funny!" observes the young student, lowering his instrument along with the corners of his mouth. He half expects to be accused of wanting to get out of practice that day, but the chances are that something really is causing a strange sound, and that you can fix it.

In a moment or two you should be able to spot the problem if you know where to start looking.

Begin by asking your child to describe his complaint. Perhaps the instrument has simply gotten out of tune.

Find out when he first noticed the problem. While he had the violin in rest position maybe his arm pressure caused the bridge to slip sideways. A violin completely "out of tune" can virtually be "popped back into tune" by returning the bridge to its central position. If he has been bothered by a strange sound all week, look elswhere.

Without being threatening, ask the child if he has tried to adjust anything on the instrument, or whether it has gotten dropped or bumped (accidently, of course!).

The following are some of the most likely problems and what to do about them:

A Buzz or Rattle When Strings are Played

Check string adjusters for a loose ring or loose tuning screw.

Be sure the adjuster lever is not touching the top of the instrument.

Some metal strings have tiny bridge-protecting tubes on them which should lie on the groove in the bridge, held in place by the string.

If one slips off the bridge it will vibrate and buzz on certain pitches.

The top or back of the instrument may have come unglued from the ribs or sides. You can detect this by knocking around the edges. Repair should be done by a violinmaker.

The chinrest may be working its way loose. One of its "leg screws" may be rattling, or it could be resting on the tailpiece and causing a vibration hum.

Black Sacconi tailguts have metal nuts concealed under the tailpiece which might be touching the top of the instrument. Slip tissue or cloth under to check.

A string may be losing its metal winding. Rub your finger lightly the length of the strings to detect a break.

In winter the wrapping around a gut string may buzz if the gut drys out. Try increasing the humidity around the instrument, or replace the string with a fresh one. Either solution may be only temporary.

Examine your childs clothing. Buttons and jewelry on sweaters and shirts can cause terrible sounds.

Something Interfering With the Response of the String

The nut at the top of the fingerboard may be worn low, placing the string too close to the fingerboard thus interfering with its free vibration. This is a job for the violinmaker. Temporary repairs calls for a tiny piece of paper or the like to be inserted between that nut and the string. Probably a job for the teacher.

Some students have tape or other substances on the fingerboard to indicate finger positions. If these are too thick, coming loose, or fraying, they will interfere with the string's vibration.

During the winter months when the instruments are very dry, the bridge will become lower, particularly on the larger instruments. Too low means the string lies almost on the fingerboard. A special bridge for each season will solve this.

The Bow Just Does Not Work Right

If the hair will not tighten it means the screw is not catching hold in the screw eyelet. One or the other may be stripped and need replacement, or perhaps the parts need a very firm hand to get them started.

With young children it is difficult to diagnose tone problems, but frequently the bow hair has become oily from hands or body. Try a heavier coat of rosin before a rehair job.

If the hair no longer resembles a broad flat ribbon, check the frog to see if the wedge of wood has come out of the ferrule. It may still be in the case and capable of being reinserted to spread the hair.

The same "bunched up" appearance occurs if the hair is twisted. Quiz your child to determine if he or a playmate removed the screw and frog, getting the latter turned before replacing it. It does happen!

"Where Are These Scratches Coming From?"

If the frog of the bow damages the top of the violin in the case, A) use an alternate bow clip, B) reverse the stick with the hair when inserting in the case, C) be sure the shoulder pad is removed from the instrument, and/or D) cover the instrument with a double thickness of flannel.

Shoulder pads with feet which grip the edges of the instrument can lose their protective rubber shoes and inflict considerable damage. The "legs" can also become bent improperly and scratch inward from the edge making long ugly scars. Be alert to these conditions, purchasing rubber replacements and using pliers to adjust the bent metal. Soap will help the new rubber shoes to slip onto the feet of the shoulderpad.

Dull Unresponsive Tone

An instrument which has been badly bumped or dropped may have had its soundpost knocked down or cracks put in its top. In either case, loosen the strings to relieve the tension on the top of the instrument and do not attempt to play it. Take it to your violinmaker promptly since its repair will require time for the glue to dry properly.

FOURTEEN

A PERSISTENT QUESTION ONE OF "TALENT"

Every parent who agrees to provide musical training wonders how his child will do. In expressing this concern, the term "talent" is frequently used. Does my child have "talent" or will he be a failure at music?

The work *talent* is defined as "a special creative or artistic *aptitude*", but in our society it is a term charged with emotion. The work *aptitude* on the other hand seems more scientific. Both terms imply a "natural ability".

When used by the layman regarding music, it almost sounds as though the child who has "talent" need only be given an instrument and a little help and music will come forth. The word *talent* would be better used if it were restricted to an indication of artistry. A good deal of technical training on an instrument would be needed before this type of *talent* could be established. And because *talent* is *creative* and *artistic* it has little to do initially with whether one has perfect pitch or strong rhythmic feelings.

Every normal human infant is born with the "natural ability" or "aptitude" to speak a language. If that baby is raised in a speechless environment, we can be certain he will not grow up speaking English. In fact, if he is not exposed to a language before a certain critical age, he may never speak anything.

Comtemporary studies lead us to believe that every child is born with an aptitude for producing music, but it will be music based on what his environment has provided him. As with language, if he has heard out-of-tune singing and blaring tones through a distorted speaker, what might be happening to his "natural ability"? If he has

- 63 -

never heard or watched a fine violinist, will he know how he should sound or look?

The experiences with music that your child has from the time of his birth will have an effect on his "aptitude". In addition, inherited characteristics such as coordination, dexterity, and sensivity to hearing will influence his adaptability to a string instrument.

Non-musical experiences play an equal part in early success. Does your child have self-discipline? Does he eagerly accept advice on how to solve a problem? Has he learned to stick with a problem until it is solved? Does he want to quit if he is not the best in a group?

In all parts of the United States scenes similar to this indicate that playing a string instrument is becoming "the thing to do!"

It is obvious that children develop at different rates when they begin an instrument. It is unjust to call one "talented" and one "inept". Perhaps the one judged best is simply a well coordinated fast reader. The other may have difficulties in this area, but years hence his sensitivity for phrasing and beautiful tone production will bring beauty to all who hear him.

A common practice is to give children what is called a musical talent test before recommending them to the public school instrumental program. Although under the circumstances there are good reasons for using these indications of a child's ability, a most perceptive reaction to this situation was given by the famous educator-violinist, Shinichi Suzuki, when he heard about it. Suzuki, whose Talent Education school is dedicated to developing the full potential of children by beginning education of high quality as early as possible, said in essence it seems to him that we wait until a child is in the fifth or sixth grade before we test him to find out if he has any natural musical ability *left!*

Parents will want to strive for that delicate balance to be achieved when their gentle, knowledgeable assistance is combined with the stimulating guidance of a good teacher. With such support, any child at any age will develop love for and skills in the art of music. You can provide your child an advantage by beginning early in such a "musically charged" environment.

SUGGESTED READING

BIRD, JOSEPH AND LOIS, *Power To The Parents! A Common Sense Psychology of Child Raising for the 70's.* Garden City, New York: Doubleday & Company, Inc., 1972.

CORSINI, RAYMOND, and PAINTER, GENEVIEVE, *The Practical Parent,* Harper and Row, 1976.

DINKMEYER, DON AND McKAY, GARY D., *Raising a Responsible Child, Practical Steps to Successful Family Relationships,* New York: Simon and Schuster, 1973.

DREIKURS, RUDOLF, with SOLTZ, VICKI, *Children: The Challenge,* New York: Hawthorn Books, Inc., 1964.

GORDON, THOMAS, *Parent Effectiveness Training, the Tested New Way To Raise Responsible Children,* New York: Peter H. Wyden, Inc., 1970.

MILLS, ELIZABETH and Parents of Students, *In the Suzuki Style,* Berkeley: Diablo Press, 1974.

SCHERL AND ROTH, INC., *You Fix Them,* Cleveland, Ohio: 1955.

SUZUKI, SHINICHI, *Nurtured By Love, A New Approach to Education,* Jericho, New York: Exposition Press, Inc., 1969.

SUZUKI, SHINICHI and Others, *The Suzuki Concept,* Berkeley, California: Diablo Press, 1973.

Most instrument Method Books contain a Preface, Introduction, or other useful information which will be of interest to parents as well as teachers.

APPENDIX

VIOLINS

Photo courtesy of Scherl and Roth

Violins are available in many sizes. Pictured here is a selection from the firm of Scherl and Roth. These violins are sold by music dealers in most major cities of the United States.

69

VIOLA

Photo courtesy of Scherl and Roth

Here is a picture of a viola beside the smaller violin for comparison.

CELLOS

Photo courtesy of Scherl and Roth

Cellos are available in different sizes for students of different ages. Shown here are three from the collection of Scherl and Roth, Cleveland.

STRING BASS

Photo courtesy of Scherl and Roth

The largest and lowest voiced instrument in the string family. The great size prevents its use by very young students, although it is indispensible to the orchestra.